International Organizations

International Courts

Boris Kolba

WORLD ALMANAC® LIBRARY

Please visit our web site at: www.worldalmanaclibrary.com
For a free color catalog describing World Almanac® Library's list
of high-quality books and multimedia programs, call 1-800-848-2928 (USA)
or 1-800-387-3178 (Canada). World Almanac® Library's fax: (414) 332-3567.

Library of Congress Cataloging-in-Publication Data

Kolba, Boris.
    International courts / by Boris Kolba.
        p. cm. — (International organizations)
    Includes bibliographical references and index.
    Contents: Disagreements among nations — Toward international justice — The World Court
at work — Disputes and decisions — International Criminal Court — The courts and the world.
    ISBN 0-8368-5519-1 (lib. bdg.)
    ISBN 0-8368-5528-0 (softcover)
    1. International courts—Juvenile literature. 2. International Court of Justice—Juvenile
literature. [1. International courts. 2. International Court of Justice.] I. Title. II. International
organizations (Milwaukee, Wis.)
    KZ6250.K65   2003
    341.5'52—dc21   2003045035

First published in 2004 by
World Almanac® Library
330 West Olive Street, Suite 100
Milwaukee, WI 53212 USA

Copyright © 2004 by World Almanac® Library.

Developed by Books Two, Inc.
Editor: Jean B. Black
Design and Maps: Krueger Graphics, Inc.: Karla J. Krueger and Victoria L. Buck
Indexer: Chandelle Black
World Almanac® Library editor: JoAnn Early Macken
World Almanac® Library art direction: Tammy Gruenewald

Photo Credits: International Court of Justice: logo, 13, 18; © AP/Wide World Photos: 17, 35,
38, 44; © AFP/CORBIS: 36; © Bettmann/CORBIS: 16, 29; © Carter Smith/CORBIS SYGMA: 30;
© Dave Bartruff/CORBIS: 14; Official DoD Photo: 8; EPA Photo Lino Arrigo Azzopardi: 28;
International Committee of the Red Cross: 10; Library of Congress: 11, 12, 32; © James Davis;
© Eye Ubiquitous/CORBIS: 4; National Archives: 34; Reuters/Benoit Doppagne: 19; Reuters/Fred
Ernst: 17; Reuters/Bazuki Muhammad: 21; Reuters/Osvaldo Rivas: 43; © Reuters News Media
Inc./CORBIS: 26; United Nations Photo Library: cover, 6, 15, 39, 40

Printed in the United States of America

1 2 3 4 5 6 7 8 9 07 06 05 04 03

TABLE OF CONTENTS

Words that appear in the glossary are printed in
boldface type the first time they occur in the text.

Disagreements among Nations

World War II raged from 1939 to 1945, engaging much of the world in brutal armed conflict. In 1946, nearly two years after the war's end, battleships and floating explosive mines still dotted the oceans. That year, four of Great Britain's warships were sailing in the Corfu Channel off the coast of Albania. Previously, the British had checked the channel for mines, which could float unseen in the water until a vessel struck them. Because they had found and removed many mines, the British believed the channel was safe.

A British warship was damaged by a floating mine in the Corfu Channel in 1946.

Sadly, they were wrong. The warships struck at least one mine. The explosion badly damaged a ship, killing forty-five sailors and officers. Great Britain claimed Albania must have known the mines were there. In the tense atmosphere, the British government blamed Albania for the damage and deaths. The unfriendly Albanian government said it was not responsible.

The conflict between Britain and Albania was alarming and dangerous. Yet **disputes** like this happen all the time in civilian life in most nations. Imagine a person who does not shovel the snow from the sidewalk in front of his or her house in the winter. A neighbor could slip on the snow and ice and fall, hurting him or herself. That person would probably say the neighbor who did not shovel was responsible—just as the British said Albania was responsible for the incident in the Corfu Channel.

When nations get into disputes like this, armed conflict and even war can break out. With its warships in the channel, Great Britain could have attacked Albania. In this case, however, the nations did not go to war. Instead, they went to court. Their dispute became the first case to be resolved by the International Court of Justice (ICJ), the world's most important international court.

What are International Courts?

Ordinary people get into disputes with each other all of the time. Sometimes people can work out their disagreements; sometimes they cannot. When people in nations like the United States or Canada have disputes they cannot resolve, they can bring them to a court. In a civil court, disputes become cases. Each person involved has a chance to explain his or her side of the case to a judge or a jury. After hearing the arguments, the judge or jury decides how to settle the dispute as fairly as possible.

When nations have conflicts they cannot resolve, they can bring their cases to an international court like the ICJ, which is often called the World Court. Here, judges consider nations' arguments and try to settle their disputes.

Comparing Civil Courts to the World Court

A civil court
- helps people settle their differences without fighting
- offers rules for people with disputes to follow
- takes time, giving people a chance to settle their arguments
- makes a decision that most people respect
- strengthens the rule of law

The World Court
- helps nations settle their differences without going to war
- offers rules for nations with arguments to follow
- takes time, giving nations a chance to resolve their own disputes
- makes a decision that much of the world respects
- strengthens international law

The judgments of the International Court of Justice can keep disputes between nations from turning into wars. Although the judges deliberate in secret, they hear the arguments of both sides in the Great Hall of Justice in a full formal court appearance, such as in this one in 2001.

International Courts like the World Court help nations resolve disputes peacefully. Disagreements between nations can turn into incredibly destructive wars. When the World Court can end an international confrontation peacefully, it saves lives and property.

These courts do more than help nations avoid war. When nations bring a case to the World Court, they must agree to follow its rules—rules designed to keep arguments orderly and calm. Also, bringing a case to an international court takes time. As nations wait for a decision, they may find their own way to settle their differences. In fact, many nations that bring **complaints** to the World Court drop them before the judges reach a decision.

In addition, international courts like the World Court have a special credibility, or acceptance as right, in much of the world. Most nations of the world—especially those involved in international organizations like the United Nations (UN)—generally accept the decisions of the World Court. This acceptance is important. With few exceptions, the international community respects actions nations take to comply with the Court's decisions.

What is International Law?

Many nations are nations of law. Their citizens live by written laws that tell them what they can and cannot do. In the international community, there are laws to guide nations. These international laws tell nations how they should behave toward each other. There are, of course, many differences between international law and the laws of nations like the United States and Canada. The two types of law also have much in common.

A nation's laws have several purposes. One is to protect people from harm. In most democratic nations, the citizens have the right to live freely and pursue their goals. That does not mean they can do anything they might want to, however. Laws help people live together without violating each other's rights. Similarly, international law spells out nations' rights and responsibilities and gives them guidelines for sharing the world peacefully.

Like people, nations have rights. They have a right to exist. They have a right to their territory, just as citizens of the United States and Canada have property rights. Nations have the right to use international waters. They also have the right to be part of the international community. They do this by sending **diplomats** to other nations.

For nations as for individuals, rights come with responsibilities. Nations are expected to respect the **sovereignty** of other nations, welcome their diplomats, and refrain from unprovoked attacks. When nations meet these expectations, the world can live in peace. When

U.S. Secretary of Defense William Cohen made a diplomatic visit to Saudi Arabia in 1998.

nations violate international laws, however, war can be the result. A body of international law exists for war as well as for peace. Nations at war must treat prisoners humanely and may not steal from one another or attack undefended cities.

International Law Differs from Laws of Nations

There are also enormous differences between international law and laws of individual nations. One is the way international law is enforced. In the United States, for example, local, state, and federal authorities enforce the law. Criminals face arrest by police and trial in criminal courts, where juries or judges can find them guilty and fine or jail them.

No police enforce international laws. International organizations of police, such as Interpol, help pursue individuals who commit crimes in one nation and flee to another. Nations, though, are policed by no one but other nations. There are no set penalties or procedures for nations that break the law. Also, while laws within many nations can be found in writing where anyone may see them, many international laws cannot.

Making International Law

In representative democracies like the United States and Canada, citizens vote for representatives who make laws at the local, state, or federal level. The representatives form legislatures to write and vote on bills, or suggested laws. An executive, such as a mayor, governor, or president, signs bills into law.

There is no "international legislature" to write bills and no executive to sign them into international law. Instead, international law comes from two main sources. The first is custom, the way most nations have always behaved. The second is treaties, formal agreements between nations. Treaties may include rules for the nations that sign the treaties, requiring them to sell each other goods or setting clear borders. Over many years, customs and treaties have grown into international law.

Treaties between Nations

Treaties generally establish specific rules for the nations that sign them to follow. Here is an example from the Jay Treaty of 1794 between the United States and Great Britain:

Article II: His Majesty will withdraw all his troops and garrisons from all posts and places within the boundary lines assigned by the treaty of peace to the United States. This evacuation shall take place on or before the first day of June, one thousand seven hundred and ninety six. . . .

Article III: No duty of entry shall ever be levied by either party on peltries brought by land or inland navigation into the said territories respectively. . . .

Toward International Justice

International law is an old idea. Seventeenth-century Dutch statesman Hugo Grotius wrote *On the Law of War and Peace*, in which he argued that all nations should follow one set of rules. He is called the "Father of International Law."

The world took few steps toward this goal until the 1800s. In 1864, a group of nations met at Geneva, Switzerland, at the urging of Henri Dunant, one of the founders of the International Red Cross. This gathering is known as the Red Cross Convention. It produced a set of rules for nations at war called the Geneva Convention.

Only twelve nations signed the convention at first. Then in 1899 and 1907, delegates met at The Hague in the Netherlands for the Hague Peace Conferences. These conferences produced more rules, moving beyond war to cover how nations could stay at peace. More nations agreed to the convention, and forty-four nations had signed by 1907.

These conferences were the true beginning of international law, but problems were obvious from the very start. First of all, how would the rules the delegates wrote be enforced? There were no international police or guaranteed punishments. In nations like Canada or France, when people break laws or have disputes, courts serve as third parties that enforce laws and resolve arguments based on the law. The delegates knew that international law would require a third party to make a final decision.

A representative of the Red Cross teaches a class of South American soldiers about international humanitarian law, which is defined in the Geneva Convention.

Treaties, Third Parties, and the First Courts

The history of international third parties reaches back to the late eighteenth century. In the 1790s, not long after the American Revolution, dangerous tensions built between Great Britain and the United States. While fighting a war with France, the British navy seized U.S. ships. The United States owed Britain money from before the American Revolution. Also, the two nations could not agree on the border between the United States and Canada.

War over these issues would have been devastating, but diplomats representing Britain and the United States were able to resolve their differences peacefully. The Jay Treaty, signed by both nations in 1794, established neutral third parties to decide each argument.

A later treaty went further, establishing an actual court. In the 1860s, the United States was torn apart by the U.S. Civil War. Britain initially agreed to remain **neutral** but later violated that agreement by selling warships to the Confederacy. After the war, the United States claimed Britain should pay for the damage done by these warships. In 1871, the nations signed the Treaty of Washington. It set up a court in Geneva to determine whether Britain was responsible. The court ordered Britain to pay $15.5 million. The success of the treaty inspired more third parties and courts.

John Jay (1745–1829)

John Jay was a New Yorker who served as president of the Continental Congress. After the United States was formed, he became the U.S. minister to Spain and later secretary of foreign affairs. Jay was the first Chief Justice of the U.S. Supreme Court in 1789. While he was Chief Justice, he crafted the Jay Treaty of 1794.

The Permanent Court of Arbitration

Third-party treaties could settle disputes between nations peacefully, but each treaty addressed only one dispute and one set of countries, leaving nothing in place for the future. The next step was a permanent court, one that could resolve one argument between two nations and continue to exist for other nations with other arguments.

Starting in the late 1890s, two U.S. secretaries of state, John Hay and Elihu Root, spoke out for a world court. Other nations were moving in the same direction. In 1899, twenty-six nations sent delegates to the First Hague Peace Conference. This meeting was the idea of Tsar Nicholas II, then the leader of Russia. His main goal for the conference was international **disarmament**. Although the world did not disarm, the conference did establish the Permanent Court of **Arbitration** (PCA) in 1900. It began operating in 1902 at The Hague.

The PCA was a huge step forward in international law, but it was not really a court. It was a list of judges, as many as four from each nation. For each case the PCA heard, a different panel was assembled from the list.

Unfortunately, the PCA had serious shortcomings. For an international dispute to be arbitrated, the nations involved had to agree to bring it to the court, approve the panel of judges, and agree in advance to abide by their decision. Nations rarely agreed with their opponents, which slowed the work of the PCA to a crawl. In 1907, a second Peace Conference met at The Hague. Forty-four

Andrew Carnegie (1835–1919)

Carnegie was a Scotland-born American businessman, entrepreneur, and philanthropist. From the huge fortune he made in steel, he donated the money for hundreds of libraries around the United States. He also donated the funds needed to build the Peace Palace, home of the PCA and the ICJ, in The Hague, Netherlands.

The Peace Palace in The Hague, Netherlands, was built to house the Permanent Court of Arbitration. Today, it is also the seat of the International Court of Justice.

nations, led by the United States, agreed to improve the PCA's rules. The U.S. secretary of state under President McKinley, Elihu Root, led an effort to turn the PCA into a real court with full-time judges. Great Britain and Germany supported the U.S. proposals, but other nations could not agree. In the end, the PCA was improved but not dramatically changed. The outbreak of World War I in 1914 made it clear, however, that the world needed stronger international courts.

Even so, the PCA was a very important development in international law. Even today, its ninety-seven national members use its judges to settle some business disputes. The World Court has joined the PCA at the Peace Palace in The Hague.

This figure of Justice is on the iron gates of the Peace Palace in The Hague.

A New International Court

International courts are meant to give nations a peaceful way to resolve disputes. World War I, known as "the war to end all wars," was strong evidence that the PCA could not achieve this. By the time the war ended in 1919, nearly sixteen million soldiers and civilians were dead. A new organization called the League of Nations was formed to prevent future wars.

President Woodrow Wilson of the United States was the driving force behind the League. As he imagined it, the League would defend each member nation. If no nation dared to face the League, Wilson believed, its members would no longer have to go to war. Part of Wilson's plan was to create a new international court that could judge any case nations brought to it. Wilson failed to persuade the American people to join the League of Nations, but when the League began in 1920, it began to draft plans for a court. The protocols (drafts of the rules and procedures) were completed and approved by the end of the year.

The Permanent Court of International Justice (PCIJ) started work at the Peace Palace in 1922. Unlike the PCA, the PCIJ was a real permanent court with a panel of full-time judges and a clear set of rules it and nations appearing before it always followed.

What Made the PCIJ Different?

As a permanent court, the PCIJ was meant to help enforce international law. People obey laws in most nations because they are enforced. When people are seen to be convicted of breaking laws, those laws take on real meaning and power. By helping to enforce international laws even to a small degree, a permanent court could encourage the world to respect those laws.

The PCIJ was different from the PCA in other ways, too. Its rules were written down so anyone could read them. Nations agreed in advance that they would work with the court. Much of its work was done in public, and all its decisions were published.

The PCIJ heard sixty-six cases and decided thirty-two of them. It also advised the League on international law, issuing twenty-seven **advisory opinions**. Yet the League and the PCIJ could not keep the world at peace. Nations like Japan and Germany left the League to pursue aggressive actions against other nations, and aggression led to war. World War II began in 1939, and the PCIJ closed in 1942.

The League of Nations was disbanded after the war ended in 1945, but the world had already begun preparing a new organization of nations to take its place. In 1942, twenty-six nations had pledged to form the United Nations. They followed through on that promise.

Creating the International Court of Justice

In April of 1945, delegates from nations around the world met in San Francisco, California, to form the UN. The plans included a new international court with new

The charter of the United Nations was signed by the representatives of fifty nations in 1945. The charter included a plan for a new International Court of Justice. At the table in the center, the delegate from Egypt is signing the actual charter.

The first session of the new International Court of Justice took place at The Hague on April 30, 1946.

jurisdiction. Every nation that joined the UN would join the court as well, thus accepting the court and, in theory, its jurisdiction. Meanwhile, a committee led by G. H. Hackworth of the United States met in Washington, D.C., to write the **statute** for the court. By the end of 1945, the UN Charter and the court's statute were both approved. The statute was based on the PCIJ statute, but the new court had a different composition and wider jurisdiction.

The International Court of Justice (ICJ—also called the CIJ, for the French *Cours Internationale de Justice*) met for the first time in April of 1946. Today, the ICJ is the world's most important international court. When people say "the World Court," they mean the ICJ.

The World Court at Work

The International Court of Justice—the "World Court"—is the **judicial** arm of the United Nations, serving all 191 member nations. Members of the UN accept the ICJ's jurisdiction and can bring complaints to the court, which also hears disputes between some nations outside the UN. The main goal of the ICJ, which it cannot always fulfill, is to peacefully resolve disputes between nations in accordance with international law.

The Court Itself

The ICJ meets at The Hague, in the Peace Palace, the same building that houses the PCA. Here, nations present their cases, the judges deliberate, and the court presents its judgments.

At the heart of the court are its fifteen judges. Each UN member nation can nominate up to four judges, two of whom may be its own citizens. The UN elects fifteen of the nominees. Judges serve nine-year

In October 2002, the UN delegates on the Security Council voted for new judges of the International Court of Justice. This is the Chinese ambassador, Yingfan Wang, casting his ballot.

International Court of Justice President Shi Jiuyong (1926–)

Judge Shi Jiuyong of China was elected president of the ICJ in 2003. Born in 1926, he has worked extensively in Chinese government. He has also studied and taught international law, both in China and abroad. He has served on the ICJ since 1994.

terms and can be reelected. Every three years, five judges' terms end, and new judges are elected.

A "new" court begins when the new or reelected judges join the ICJ. A new court elects its own president and vice president. In 2003, the ICJ elected Judge Shi Jiuyong of China to be its president and Judge Raymond Ranjeva of Madagascar to be vice president. Judge Thomas Buergenthal from the United States joined the court in 2000. No other judge from the United States may join the court until at least 2009, when Buergenthal's term ends.

Rules and Registry, Advice and Judgments

The ICJ's rules are designed to ensure that the court represents the world as fairly as possible. Judges are elected from a wide range of nations, and no more than one judge at a time from any one nation can serve on the court. Most important, judges are required to remain neutral. They must decide each case fairly rather than acting for their own nations.

The ICJ does more than resolve international disputes. Its judges also serve as authorities on international law. In this role, they advise the UN and other international organizations on international law. Since 1945, the ICJ has issued twenty-two advisory opinions. A very important advisory opinion that the court issued in 1996 declared that nuclear weapons were illegal and should be destroyed.

Most of the people who work at the ICJ make up the court's Registry. This is like the secretariat in some other organizations, consisting of officials who organize cases, keep the court's records, set its budget, and issue press releases.

A Court for Nations

Although there are similarities, the ICJ is very different from courts in nations like the United States and Canada. A key difference is that United States and Canadian courts serve people. They sometimes hear cases involving groups or businesses, but in general, they deal with individuals. The ICJ, on the other hand, serves nations. Only nations can bring complaints to the ICJ, and the court will only hear their cases against other nations. If an individual tried to bring a dispute to the ICJ, he or she would be turned away. There are no exceptions.

To bring a complaint to the ICJ, a nation must be a party to the court. It must accept the court's statute, agreeing that the court has the right to resolve the dispute and that it will abide by the court's rules. Parties to the court also agree to accept the judges' decisions, even if those decisions are against their interests. All nations in the UN are automatically parties to the ICJ. Nonmember nations can use the court by agreeing to the statute and accepting responsibilities such as helping to pay for the

In 1998, this woman demonstrated outside NATO headquarters in Brussels, Belgium, because NATO has paid no attention to the World Court's advisory opinion saying that nuclear weapons are illegal. Her mask simulates radiation burns.

ICJ. On occasion, nations are allowed to take a case to the court without agreeing to the statute if they agree to follow the court's rules and accept its judgment.

How Does a Dispute End Up Before a Court?

The ICJ cannot just take over when an argument breaks out between nations. One or more nations must bring a case to the ICJ, just as cases are brought to courts in the legal systems of most countries. In an American or Canadian court, one person, usually with a lawyer, files a complaint, or formal charge, explaining his or her side of the dispute. The court issues a **summons** to the other party, telling him or her that a complaint has been filed. That other party responds with his or her side. These are the first steps to having the court hear the case.

The process at the ICJ is somewhat different. Nations do not file complaints, and the ICJ cannot issue summonses. Instead, both nations involved in a dispute must agree to bring it to the court. Without this agreement in some form, the ICJ cannot take a case. The simplest way to have a case heard is for both nations involved to agree to bring a case to the ICJ. Representatives of the nations write the agreement, explaining what issues they want the court to decide. The agreement is submitted to the ICJ, thus giving it jurisdiction.

Cases can arrive at the ICJ through other channels as well. One possibility is through a treaty. Some treaties specify how the nations signing it will resolve future disputes. If the treaty says the ICJ will settle future conflicts, the nations give the ICJ jurisdiction when they sign the treaty. In addition, nations can formally declare that they will accept the court's jurisdiction in any international conflicts involving specific issues.

In situations where a nation has agreed in advance, through a treaty or declaration, to accept the ICJ's jurisdiction, another nation can file an application without a new agreement. The application is similar to a complaint in a U.S. or Canadian court. The ICJ does not issue a summons, however; the other nation is simply expected to respond. Ideally, a nation that has agreed to accept the ICJ's jurisdiction will respond to another nation's application. But sometimes nations do not respond. Nations have claimed there were exceptions to their agreements and they have simply ignored applications. The ICJ cannot do much about this lack of response.

In a public ceremony in 2003, officials from Malaysia and Singapore agreed—after many years of quarreling—to ask the World Court to settle their territorial dispute over some land they both claimed.

How Does the ICJ Hear Cases?

The biggest differences between the ICJ and courts within nations are in the ways they decide cases. Regular court cases generally require lawyers to represent both sides and explain their legal positions. Lawyers must complete studies at law schools and pass a test called the bar examination in order to understand both the laws and the legal procedures.

Nations appearing at the ICJ have representatives called agents, but a nation's representative need not be a lawyer. Agents do not need any special license. Nations generally choose experts on international law and the ICJ as their agents. Once both parties have chosen agents and notified the court of their choices, a case before the ICJ can begin.

Each side presents its side of the argument. At the ICJ, this happens in two steps. First, each side presents a written argument focusing on the issues on which the nations disagree. Written arguments can be complex and full of detail. They take time to prepare, to read, and to understand.

The judges and all parties read the written arguments. Sometimes, nations write responses to each other's arguments—and even responses to responses. All of these documents, including the initial arguments, are called pleadings. Because the written stage includes all of the pleadings, it can take a very long time to finish, often years.

The next step of the case is oral arguments. For this stage, the entire court meets publicly at the Peace Palace, in a room known as the Great Hall of Justice. The judges wear black robes, and agents dress in the formal clothes of their nations. The agents present their cases out loud before the judges.

The oral stage usually takes two or three weeks. Each agent makes his or her argument in a speech that is planned and written ahead of time.

Some ICJ Facts

The ICJ has two official languages, French and English.

Nations can object to a complaint. Often, one nation argues that the ICJ does not have jurisdiction to hear a particular case.

Many cases that begin before the ICJ do not end with a decision by the judges. Instead, the nation bringing the case decides to drop it, or both parties resolve the conflict on their own.

All notes made by the judges as they discuss a case are destroyed by the ICJ.

Few witnesses ever appear. Those who do are generally experts on international law rather than people who actually saw disputed events. Judges may ask the agents questions, but they usually do so in writing. The proceeding is much more formal than a civil court trial.

Making a Decision

After oral arguments, the judges think, discuss, and make their decision. The Peace Palace includes a Deliberation Room where the judges deliberate, or discuss, cases in secret. First, they study all the arguments and discuss their first reactions. The president of the court helps the judges identify the particular issues that they must decide.

The World Court judges prepared in 1999 to hear the arguments of the former Yugoslavia in the case it brought against ten NATO countries to make them stop their air attacks.

Next, each judge writes his or her opinion on the disputed issues. The judges read each other's opinions and discuss them until they reach a consensus, or general agreement, on enough of the issues to begin writing a decision to explain what the nations must do to resolve their differences peacefully. Decisions are often long and complicated documents. After drafting a decision, the judges read it and revise it, voting after each revision. When a majority approves, the decision is final.

The last step is the public presentation of the decision. It is read aloud to the nations' representatives and reporters. The UN is notified. Decisions of the ICJ are binding; each party to a case is expected to follow the court's orders. Nations, however, do not always live up to their obligations. Nonetheless, the decisions are often momentous events in international relations.

Disputes and Decisions

Since it began in 1945, the ICJ has heard many cases and made many decisions. At their best, the court's decisions have contributed to international law and made it easier for nations to settle disputes peacefully. The least effective decisions have been ignored or have sparked further conflict. The international impact of ICJ cases makes them very different from cases heard in national, provincial, or state courts. Yet most of the cases follow patterns that can be found in these nations' courts.

Disputes Over Territory: Borders

Many of the cases the ICJ hears deal with international borders. They follow a pattern similar to disagreements between neighbors over the location of the line between their properties. Neighbors arguing over property lines often do end up in regular courts. Nations have similar disputes with their neighbors, disagreeing about where their borders are. Many such disagreements have been heard by the ICJ.

The Minquiers and Ecrehos case is one example. Minquiers and Ecrehos are groups of islands between the United Kingdom and France.

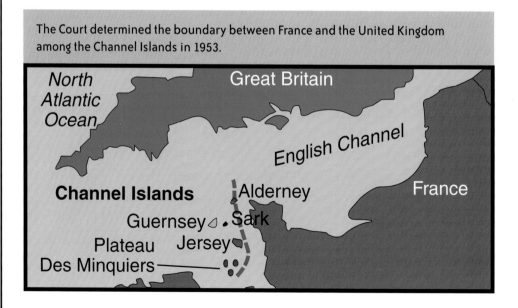

The Court determined the boundary between France and the United Kingdom among the Channel Islands in 1953.

The two nations had argued over who owned the islands since the Norman Conquest of 1066—nearly nine hundred years! In 1953, the ICJ concluded that the islands were British. Both nations accepted the decision, settling the dispute peacefully.

The Frontier Dispute case between Burkina Faso and Mali also began with an argument over a border. In the 1980s, these neighboring African nations were unable to agree who controlled a region called the Agacher Strip. The conflict led to violence. Although the case had already begun at the ICJ in 1983, the nations fought a short war over the Agacher Strip in 1985.

The battle started on Christmas Day of 1985 and lasted for five days. As the fighting ended, both nations requested that the ICJ put measures in place to keep the peace. In January 1986, the court issued an order that included a cease-fire. Mali and Burkina Faso respected the order, and the judges proceeded to study the history of the region. The court drew a clear border between the two nations' territories that both nations accepted. In this difficult case, the ICJ was successful.

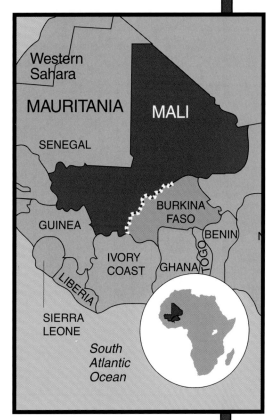

Disputes Over Territory: Oceans and Fishing Rights

A nation's territory can extend past its land. Maritime nations have direct access to the world's oceans; their ships can easily sail around the world. These nations often claim territory in the oceans, including islands. In December of 2001, the South American maritime nation of Nicaragua

In 2001, Colombian soldiers patrolled the beaches of San Andrés, part of a group of Caribbean islands in a case pending before the ICJ. Nicaragua claims an area of waters that includes the islands.

came to the ICJ with a complaint against its neighbor, Colombia. Nicaragua claimed that the islands of San Andrés and Providencia, which are controlled by Colombia, are part of its territory. The case will probably not be decided until at least 2005.

Territorial conflict is especially common in ocean areas where fish are plentiful. In maritime nations, ocean fish are a key part of people's diets and of the economy. Most such nations take charge of the waters off their coasts, making rules to control fishing there. Maritime nations often argue over which waters belong to which country.

International arguments over fishing rights are similar to those over nations' borders. They are also like certain types of property disputes often seen in local courts. When neighbors share a resource located on one neighbor's property, the other neighbor needs an easement, which is a right to use someone else's land for one purpose. Individual property owners often argue over easements, sometimes taking those arguments to court.

Disputes between international neighbors over fishing rights are similar, and the ICJ has heard several of them. One that the court settled was a dispute between the United Kingdom and Norway. These maritime nations share access to the North and Norwegian Seas. In 1935, Norway declared that some fisheries in these seas were off limits to British fishing boats. The argument dragged on for years, finally reaching the ICJ in 1949. In 1951, the court reached its *Fisheries* decision, only its second decision. It announced that Norway had the right to keep the British—and everyone else— from fishing in these waters.

The ICJ often considers other issues similar to easements. In the 1950s, Portugal held colonies within the territory of India. Portugal claimed the right to go through India's territory to reach its colonies. The ICJ decided Portugal had the right to pass through—a right similar to an easement—but it excluded Portugal's military from that right.

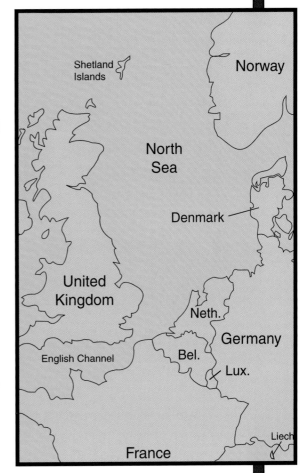

Disputes Over Territory: The Continental Shelf

A nation's territory can reach below the oceans. After all, land does not simply end at the ocean shore. It slopes gradually down under water for a few hundred feet or for many miles. This slope is the continental shelf, and nations have argued over who controls it. In 1969, the ICJ settled cases over the continental shelf shared by Germany and two of its neighbors, Denmark and the Netherlands. The court issued an order explaining how to split the use of the shelf among the three nations.

The harbor at Valletta, the ancient capital of Malta, shows how low-lying the island is. It lies above the continental shelf of North Africa. In 1985, the International Court of Justice decided how the shelf is to be shared by Libya and Malta.

A similar dispute arose between Libya and Malta, an island nation to the north of Libya that shares a portion of continental shelf with it. The ICJ studied the coasts of the nations, the distance between them, and the shelf itself. In 1985, the court settled the case by defining which areas of the continental shelf belonged to which nation.

Disputes over the Rights of Citizens

The ICJ also hears many cases dealing with the rights of citizens. In nations like the United States and Canada, citizens have clearly spelled-out rights that their governments are required to respect. If their rights are violated, citizens can resolve the problem in court. People have rights in international law as well, although they are not as clearly defined as in national law. When international rights are violated, nations can bring their complaints to the ICJ.

Most of these disputes arise when citizens of one nation live for long periods in other nations. If they are mistreated by their host nations, conflicts can and do break out. One of these came early in the ICJ's history. In 1948, France placed limits on some business deals in its colony of Morocco that affected U.S. citizens living there. The United States complained to the ICJ that its citizens in Morocco should not have to follow France's rules or pay its taxes. The ICJ ruled for France.

This is not a very dramatic example, but some cases have been very dramatic. In 1979, the nation of Iran was swept by a revolution. The United States embassy in the capital of Tehran was taken over by an armed group of students who held fifty-two U.S. citizens prisoner. This was a very serious violation of their rights. The United States government tried everything in its power to free them, including bringing the case to the ICJ.

The ICJ agreed with the United States. The court found that under international law, Iran owed protection to the embassy's personnel. Not only had it failed to protect them, it would not release them.

At the American embassy in Iran, fifty-two American citizens, including this blindfolded woman being led by an Iranian student, were held prisoner for 444 days starting in 1979. The International Court of Justice declared that Iran had taken away the hostages' rights.

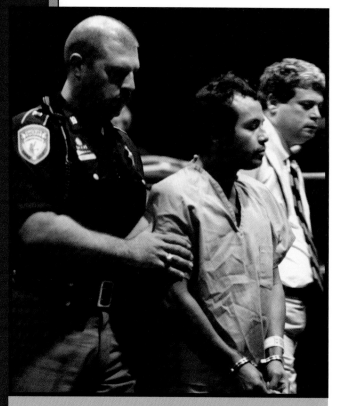

Mexico brought a case before the ICJ accusing the United States of not letting Mexican citizens found guilty of murder contact Mexican consular officials. In 2003, the Court told the United States to prevent executions while it considered the case.

Indeed, Iran even refused to appear before the ICJ. The case served the purpose of clarifying and reaffirming international law, but the ICJ could not free the hostages. In this case, the ICJ was unable to promote peace and international justice.

Even so, the ICJ continues to hear such cases. In 2003, Mexico brought a case against the United States. Mexico charged that fifty-four Mexican citizens had been sentenced to death in several U.S. states without diplomatic officials having contact with the prisoners. Mexico claims that this lack of contact is in violation of the Vienna Convention on **Consular** Relations, which describes the expected functions of a nation's consular offices.

International Business Disputes

Other disputes that often wind up before the ICJ involve international businesses. This should not be a surprise because most national courts hear many cases arising from business. People claim that businesses have caused them harm, businesses accuse one another of treating each other unfairly, and governments charge companies with breaking laws that regulate businesses.

National conflicts over business are not uncommon, and when people from one nation do business in another, international conflicts can arise. The business disputes the ICJ deals with tend to be similar to cases in national courts. One—the Barcelona Traction, Light and Power Company, Limited case—dragged on for twelve years. Barcelona Traction was based in Canada but operated in Spain, where it ran out of money. The Spanish government seized its property, which angered the owners.

Similar cases reach regular courts whenever companies run out of money and go bankrupt. The people who owned the failed businesses try to get their investments back, but often many other people are owed money. Everyone involved fights over what is left. The owners of Barcelona Traction fought with Spain. The owners were Belgian citizens living in Canada, so they turned to their native country to take action at the ICJ. Belgium charged that Spain had dealt unfairly with Barcelona Traction. The case began at the ICJ in 1958 and finally ended in 1970. The court decided that what Spain did was none of Belgium's business.

Another international business case started in 1987 when an Italian company named Raytheon-Elsi went out of business and Italy seized its factory. Raytheon-Elsi's owners—other companies from the United States—pressed their government to take action at the ICJ. The United States charged that Italy's actions violated a 1948 treaty between the two nations. In 1989, the court denied the U.S. charges.

Disputes Between Neighboring Nations

The world is a small place in which nations exist side by side. Many cases the ICJ hears stem from actions nations take that affect—and sometimes harm—their neighbors. The conflicts that result are similar to disputes between neighbors in many countries. The citizens of these nations have the right to do almost anything on their own property that isn't against the law. But when people fail to take care of their property or do dangerous things there, they can harm their neighbors.

The Corfu Channel case that began this book is one such conflict between international neighbors. Great Britain's ships had struck a mine in Albanian waters, and the British government claimed that Albania was responsible. In 1949, the ICJ decided the case in favor of the British. Corfu was Albania's responsibility, the court said. Even if Albania did not put the mines there, it had to keep the channel safe. Albania had to pay Great Britain for the damage the mines caused.

Some of these cases have been difficult and controversial for the ICJ. Nations do not like to be told what they can and cannot do. In 1973, France announced that it would test nuclear weapons in the South Pacific during the next year. The French plan was to explode nuclear bombs in the atmosphere. Australia and New Zealand, two nations in the South Pacific region, were very angry about the tests. Nuclear explosions release dangerous radiation, and these nations' governments believed that winds would carry the radiation into their territories, harming their people and the environment.

Nuclear explosions release dangerous radiation that can drift long distances. This fact worried Australia and New Zealand when France planned atmospheric tests in the South Pacific in 1974. France ignored the World Court's request that it wait until the court could consider the matter.

France's actions can be compared to those of a business that stores dangerous chemicals near a residential neighborhood. The residents can get very upset and might take the business to court. This is exactly what Australia and New Zealand did—they brought their complaint to the ICJ. The court ordered France not to test any bombs until it reached a decision, but the French government claimed the ICJ did not have jurisdiction over the matter. France did not send representatives to the hearings, and in 1974, it went ahead with the tests.

This kind of defiance cast doubt on the power of the ICJ to resolve international disputes. In this case, the court was able to preserve some of its standing when France said the 1974 tests would be its last. Because Australia and New Zealand were trying to prevent the tests, the court decided the case could be dropped. In 1995, however, the French government announced a new round of nuclear tests. New Zealand renewed its complaint. The ICJ was in a very difficult position. France's actions directly undermined the court's authority. The ICJ ducked the issue. Because new tests were to be done underground, the court refused to take the case.

Other cases have been even more difficult. In the 1980s, the government of the Central American nation Nicaragua was faced with armed rebellion from groups called *contras*. Nicaragua believed the United States was supporting the contras, and in 1984, it charged the United States with being illegally involved in its national affairs. The ICJ began considering the case and ordered the United States not to interfere.

Nicaragua presented its arguments in 1985, but U.S. representatives did not appear before the court. The U.S. government claimed that the ICJ did not have jurisdiction and that the case was not legitimate. The case continued, but without U.S. cooperation, it became increasingly frustrating. What could the ICJ do to enforce its orders? By 1991, Nicaragua dropped its charges.

Cases like this one make clear the limitations of the ICJ and of international law and courts in general. They depend on the cooperation of powerful nations. What happens to international courts when those nations do not cooperate?

Chapter Five

International Criminal Court

The ICJ is the most significant international court; when people speak of the "World Court," they refer to the ICJ. Yet there are crucial areas of international law that the World Court cannot address. Key among these are the terrible crimes sometimes committed during wars between nations. Only nations can appear before the ICJ, but individuals are responsible for the crimes of war. The ICJ is unable to do much of anything about **war crimes,** no matter how horrifying they are. As José Ayala Lasso, the former UN High Commissioner for Human Rights, has said, "A person stands a better chance of being tried and judged for killing one human being than for killing 100,000."

What is International Crime?

The International Criminal Court is intended to deal with international crime. Mostly, this means war crimes. If soldiers intentionally attack civilians—not other soldiers—the act is a war crime. International crime also includes crimes against humanity, such as forcing large numbers of citizens from their homes, turning them into refugees. **Genocide,** or mass extermination, is also a crime against humanity. The Holocaust of World War II, in which the Nazi government of Germany tried to kill all the Jewish people in Europe, was a case of genocide. When the Allies liberated some Nazi concentration camps in 1945, they found only a few starving prisoners, such as the ones above. Millions of other Jews had been put to death. Some of the top Nazis were tried for their war crimes in the Nuremberg Trials.

A memorial to the genocide that took place in Rwanda in 1994 shows the remains of only a few of the several hundred thousand ethnic Tutsis killed by the ethnic Hutu majority. In 1998, some Rwandan officials were found guilty of such murders in a special international criminal tribunal.

There may be a solution, however. In July of 2002, a new court was established at The Hague. The purpose of the International Criminal Court (ICC) is to hold individuals who commit crimes of war and other international crimes responsible for their actions. Unlike the ICJ, it can put people on trial and punish them by sending them to prison.

The History of the ICC

In the twentieth century, the international community made many efforts to punish people who committed international crimes. After World War II, a special court met at Nuremberg, Germany, to put that

Wanted by Interpol

MILOSEVIC, Slobodan

22 March 2000

Home
Interpol
Wanted
Search
Recent
Trafficking in Human Beings
Criminal Intelligence Analysis
Drugs
Payment cards
Forensic
Help
Search

Legal Status	
Present family name:	**MILOSEVIC**
Forename:	**SLOBODAN**
Sex:	MALE
Date of birth:	20 August 1941 (58 years old)
Place of birth:	POZAREVAC - SERBIA, YUGOSLAVIA
Language spoken:	ENGLISH , SERBO CROAT
Nationality:	YUGOSLAVIA

Physical description

Interpol—the International Criminal Police Organization—sent out a wanted notice for the arrest of Slobodan Milosevic, who had been president of the former Yugoslavia. He is the highest ranking person to be tried by the International Criminal Tribunal for Yugoslavia.

nation's Nazi leaders on trial for killing millions of Jews in concentration camps. A similar tribunal, or deciding body, tried the leaders of Japan for their conduct during the war. In the 1990s, the UN established special tribunals to try and punish people who committed war crimes in the former Yugoslavia and in the African nation of Rwanda. In 1998, the first verdict of genocide was brought against a number of Rwandans—mostly ethnic Hutus—for the killing of perhaps half a million Tutsi people.

The International Criminal Tribunal for Yugoslavia (ICTY), established by the UN in 1993, has been even more influential. Yugoslavia was a nation in Eastern Europe that fell apart in the early 1990s after the collapse of the Soviet Union. Sections of Yugoslavia, such as Bosnia, Croatia, and Kosovo, wanted to become separate nations. Their efforts led to a civil war during which countless war crimes—including genocide—were committed. The ICTY has attempted to punish the people responsible; the tribunal has put many people on trial and sent many of them to prison. Most important, Slobodan Milosevic, the former president of Yugoslavia, has been charged with having his followers kill countless civilians. In 2003, his trial was still proceeding.

> ## The Universal Declaration of Human Rights
>
> The Universal Declaration of Human Rights outlines key rights that belong to all people in all the world's nations. It was drafted by a UN committee chaired by U.S. delegate and former First Lady Eleanor Roosevelt and approved without dissent in December of 1948. Although the Declaration is not a legally binding treaty, it established a guiding principle for international law—that there are human rights no government or individual should be permitted to violate.

Throughout the twentieth century, the nations of the world had discussed the idea of an international court to judge war crimes. In December of 1948, the UN's General Assembly voted to adopt the Universal Declaration of Human Rights as well as a resolution defining genocide and calling for punishment for it. Member nations requested a formal study of the possibility of establishing an international criminal court. By 1954, however, the effort had been abandoned.

The idea refused to die, and in 1989, UN member nation Trinidad and Tobago formally proposed the establishment of an International Criminal Court, or ICC. This time, the UN asked its experts on international law to write an actual plan for a permanent criminal court. The plan was finally presented to the world in the summer of 1998.

The Rome Statute, named for the Italian city that hosted the conference at which the plan was presented, was the most important development in international law since the founding of the ICJ. It set guidelines for a permanent court with jurisdiction over genocide, crimes against humanity, and other war crimes. The court would only be able to

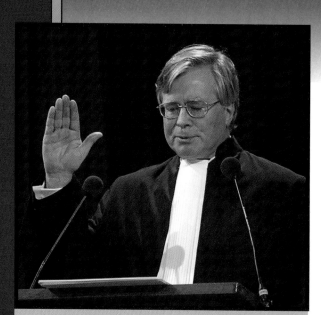

The ICC was inaugurated on March 11, 2003. Philippe Kirsch of Canada was sworn in as a judge and then elected the court's first president.

charge individuals if their native nations proved unable or unwilling to do so. The court would have eighteen judges serving nine-year terms like the judges of the ICJ. The statute included rules for investigations, trials, penalties, and appeals.

The Rome conference drew 160 nations. In July of 1998, they approved the statute in an overwhelming vote. The next step in forming the ICC was for nations to ratify, or formally approve, the statute. For the court to be established, at least sixty nations had to ratify the statute. The first nation to do so was Sénégal in February of 1999. By April of 2002, the sixty-nation mark had been reached. The Rome Statute went into effect that July. Judges were nominated by the end of 2002; eighteen were elected in early 2003. The judges were inaugurated at The Hague on March 11, 2003.

The ICC and the United States

Before its judges could even be seated, the ICC encountered a serious challenge. The United States had voted to approve the Rome Statute in July of 1998. Even as U.S. President Bill Clinton signed the statute, however, he expressed concerns about the ICC. The president and members of the U.S. Congress worried that the ICC could be used by other nations to hurt the United States. Could nations use the ICC to bring false charges against Americans? Would Americans be unfairly attacked at the court?

Because the United States was and is the world's most powerful nation, critics of the ICC argued, its military personnel served in many

On April 21, 2003, the representatives of the eighty-nine member countries belonging to the newly established International Criminal Court met at the United Nations to elect the court's first chief prosecutor. They chose an Argentinian lawyer, Luis Moreno Ocampo.

parts of the world. The critics feared that military personnel would be especially vulnerable to prosecution at the ICC and that other nations might resent U.S. power and use the ICC to get back at the United States somehow. These concerns left U.S. ratification of the Rome Statute in doubt. President Clinton still favored ratification.

Bill Clinton did not remain president, however. George W. Bush, who became U.S. president in 2001, was opposed to the ICC. He announced that the United States would not ratify the Rome Statute; in fact, the nation backed out of its initial approval. The statute went into effect without American support. Furthermore, the U.S. government argued that because it was not a party to the statute, the ICC has no jurisdiction over its citizens. It would not participate in any ICC cases and did not send representatives to the inauguration of the court in 2003.

Supporters of the ICC say the U.S. objections are groundless. They point out that the statute has safeguards to prevent frivolous or malicious prosecutions. Whether the United States has any real reasons to worry about the ICC, its refusal to cooperate places the new court at a serious disadvantage. Its authority was challenged by the world's most powerful nation before it heard a single case. Without U.S. support, it is not certain that the ICC can have an impact on international crime.

Chapter Six

The Courts and the World

Kofi Annan (standing), secretary-general of the United Nations, celebrated the fiftieth anniversary of the Universal Declaration of Human Rights with the ICJ in 1998.

The ICJ was in its fifty-fourth year as the twenty-first century began. In this new century, the international court system faced—and continues to face—new challenges. International law continues to grow and evolve; powerful nations, including the United States, continue to cast doubt on the authority of courts like the ICJ and the ICC. It is difficult to look ahead and see just what place these international courts will have in the world in the future.

International Courts and International Law

The history of international courts is closely tied to the history of international law. Both have similar goals: to protect the rights of nations and their citizens and to keep the world as peaceful as possible. International courts and international law have shared success and failure. What is their relationship today, and what will it be in the future?

Today, international courts interpret, define, and even strengthen international law. As they deliberate and decide cases, courts like the ICJ determine how these laws will be applied to the nations of the world. Furthermore, their decisions give international law more authority. Each time a court makes use of this body of law, it takes on greater practical weight in the world.

Despite the work of international courts, however, international law is only as strong as the nations of the world allow it to be. If a nation violates international law, what can the world do? There are no international police to arrest the offender. International courts cannot force the nation to appear for a trial. Even if a complaint is brought to the ICJ, the nation named in the complaint might claim the court has no jurisdiction over the matter and ignore it. What happens then? It may seem the only option is war against the lawbreaking nation, but international law is supposed to prevent war, not encourage it.

When nations consistently ignore the decisions made by international courts, the courts lose their authority. International law is weakened. Both the laws and courts become less important. Nations can make them stronger by using and respecting them. Each time nations bring cases to the courts and respect their decisions, both the courts and the laws are strengthened. If all the nations of the world follow this course in the future, international law and courts can work together toward their common goals with greater success.

The ICJ's Advisory Cases

In addition to hearing cases, the ICJ gives advice on international law to organizations such as the UN, the United Nations Educational, Scientific, and Cultural Organization (UNESCO), and the World Health Organization (WHO). When these organizations have trouble making sense of international law, they turn to the ICJ. The court issues advisory opinions explaining the law and how it should be applied.

International Courts and National Power: Striking a Balance

International courts have had trouble working with nations. To resolve international disputes, these courts have to order nations to do things the individual nations do not want to do. Furthermore, the courts order governments to do things that might hurt their citizens. When the ICJ decides against a nation, for example, it might demand a fine that would come out of the nation's budget and its people's taxes. Few nations are eager to give up any of their authority or sovereignty to work with international courts.

Nations need sovereignty to lead their people; without it, their governments may lose the respect of their citizens. When nations try to resolve international disputes without giving any ground, tensions generally escalate. When nations confront one another but want to avoid war, there are really only two possible courses of action: one nation can back down, or both nations can give up authority over the matter by bringing the case to an international court. Otherwise, international confrontations can spiral into wars.

To work with international courts and to prevent war, nations must give up some of their sovereignty. Each must strike a balance. How much sovereignty should a nation give up, and how much can it keep? These questions are most complicated for the world's most powerful nation, the United States.

International Courts and National Power: The United States

The respect and cooperation of the United States can give international courts their greatest strength. For a number of reasons, that respect and cooperation have not always been offered. The power of the United States gives it enormous authority in the international community. When it gives sovereignty to international courts like the ICJ or the ICC, its own influence is softened. The controversy over the ICC demonstrates that the U.S. government worries that less powerful nations might use the courts to diminish its authority.

These concerns have brought the United States into conflict with international courts. As was mentioned previously, in 1984, Nicaragua accused

Although the ICJ makes decisions in many types of cases, its primary purpose is to help nations avoid armed conflict. In 2000, this soldier guarded a base in northern Nicaragua.

the United States of supporting armed groups opposed to its government. The ICJ took the case, but the United States refused to accept the court's jurisdiction or take part in any way. Its refusal to be a party to the ICC has greatly widened the distance between the United States and the international court system.

Because of its power, a split with the United States has a much greater impact on international courts than a split with any other nation. The authority of the courts is seriously threatened by the absence of the United States from the court. U.S. power has often been a very positive force in the world. International courts can also be a powerful force for peace and stability—if they have real authority. A strong court system, like strong international law, has the potential to do a great deal for international peace and justice. It is doubtful, however, that this can happen without the United States.

What Does the Future Hold?
International courts could help strengthen international law and preserve peace in the world. Yet the courts need the help of the world's

The World Court succeeds when the world accepts its verdicts. Here, officials from Qatar prepare to hear the 2001 verdict of their case against Bahrain concerning the boundary among islands in the Persian Gulf.

nations. To do their jobs, the ICJ and the ICC need nations to give up some authority and sovereignty—a big price for nations to pay. The United States has clashed with the ICJ and withdrawn support from the ICC. The future holds both great promise for international courts and the very real possibility that they may become irrelevant and could fail.

There is every indication that in the twenty-first century, the world will need strong international courts more than ever. Many nations show little or no respect for international law; a stronger ICJ may encourage these nations to respect their neighbors' rights. The stability of the world is threatened by international terrorism; the ICC may provide a means to try and punish terrorists. Yet international courts have serious weaknesses. They work slowly, and they are not always able to command the respect of the world's nations. Relying on them for peace and justice could make the world more dangerous, not less.

Somewhere in between, there may be a good answer. International courts could continue to help nations resolve disputes without going to war. International law could grow into a stronger force for peace. Nations could keep the authority they need to protect themselves and each other in times of crisis. Perhaps this is what the future holds.

Time Line

1794 The United States and Great Britain sign the Jay Treaty, agreeing to use a third party to resolve their disputes.

1864 The Geneva Conventions establish international ideals of behavior in war.

1871 The United States and Great Britain sign the Treaty of Washington, agreeing to set up a special court to resolve certain disputes.

1899 Nations at the First Hague Peace Conference agree to start the Permanent Court of Arbitration.

1902 The Permanent Court of Arbitration starts at The Hague.

1907 Second Peace Conference is held at The Hague; the rules of the Permanent Court of Arbitration are revised.

1919 World War I ends; the League of Nations is planned.

1920 The League of Nations begins; the League starts work on rules for a new, permanent World Court.

1922 The Permanent Court of International Justice starts at The Hague.

1942 While fighting World War II, twenty-two nations pledge to form the United Nations.

1945 World War II ends; the United Nations is founded and begins work on a new World Court; war crimes tribunal begins at Nuremberg, Germany.

1946 The International Court of Justice starts at The Hague.

1949 The International Court of Justice issues its first decision.

1985 Nicaragua charges the United States with supporting armed rebels; the United States refuses to recognize the International Court of Justice's authority to decide the case.

1989 Planning for the International Criminal Court (ICC) begins.

1993 The International Criminal Tribunal for Yugoslavia is established by the United Nations.

1998 The United Nations approves the plan for the ICC.

2001 The United States withdraws its support for the ICC.

2003 The International Criminal Court becomes fully operational.

Glossary

advisory opinion an opinion written by the judges of the court that offers advice on a point of international law

arbitration a hearing and decision in a matter in which both sides agree to accept the decision

civil court a court of law that resolves disputes between people, businesses, and sometimes government agencies

complaint a formal charge, filed with a court of law, that a person or group has violated the complainer's rights or broken a law

consular representing the interests of the citizens of one country in another

diplomat a person who represents his or her own nation in its relationships with other nations

disarmament the process by which a nation rids itself of some or all of its weapons and military capacity

dispute an argument or disagreement

genocide the mass murder or attempted mass murder of all members of a particular racial, ethnic, religious, or cultural group

judicial having to do with judges and courts

jurisdiction the authority of a particular court to resolve a particular type of dispute

neutral belonging to neither one side nor the other

sovereignty absolute authority; freedom from any higher or outside authority

statute a document formally stating a law or laws, or the rules governing a government body or court

summons a formal order requiring someone to appear before a court of law

war crimes violations of the international laws governing warfare, especially the deliberate killing of civilians

BOOKS

Carter, Jimmy. *Talking Peace: A Vision for the Next Generation*. Dutton Children's Books, 1995.

Rice, Earle Jr. *The Nuremberg Trials*. Famous Trials Series. Lucent Books, 1998.

ADDRESSES AND WEB SITES

Coalition for the International Criminal Court
c/o WFM/CICC
777 UN Plaza
New York, NY 10017
USA
www.iccnow.org/

International Criminal Court
Division of Common Services
P.O. Box 19519
2500 CM The Hague
The Netherlands

International Court of Justice
Peace Palace
2517 KJ The Hague
The Netherlands
www.icj-cij.org/icjwww/icj002.htm

Permanent Court of Arbitration
Peace Palace
2517 KJ The Hague
The Netherlands
www.pca-cpa.org/

Index